I0061183

Democracy Mutual Aid
Response to project 2025

(Neurodivergent Quality
of Life Graph)
Written by Russell
Griffith - Chandler
Copyright © 2025

INTIFF LLC

ISBN: 979-8-218-67937-8 (paperback)

Chapters

Democracy
Mutual Aid

(Neurodiverge nt Quality of Life Graph)

Introduction

First I love to thank Novantoro as my illustrator of most of my books and Novantoro remade my Neurodivergent Graph to a better looking

design with the same concept. For this book I
illustrated the cover.
As a black person I believe it is important to
decolonize our mind, body and soul and our
environment. One way I decolonize my mind is
to give myself an African name. This was a
rebirth. My new name is Osmala Chinga.

I made anarchist Decentralized voting
structures so that many minorities such as
Queer people of color can have more of a say
in their votes. Often people make rules on the
majority which sometimes is the dominant
ignorant population of social issues and
disabilities. Majority population may be
ignorant by whatever reason, usually a product
of religion, and economic conditions of the
time.

Many people say Russell. He knows

nothing about nothing. Well, I am smart

and a self-taught philosopher like

Aristotle, Socrates and Plato. I do not

have a degree yet. I am unmatched to

my right. I am black and disabled, but I

am like Helen Keller. I'm like David

Hume who dropped out of college. We

don't need degrees for everything. I

have an entrepreneur certificate and I'm

happy with that. Some people can't

afford degrees. Russell Griffith -

Chandler is brave, bold and intelligent.

Russells non colonial name is Osamala.

Since the mention of project 2025 he

has been teaming up with organizations

to fight this crime to humanity. This book

is a response to project 2025.

The shallow naysayers are just toxic critical voices whose words need to be used as toilet paper.

People say all Russell is going to do is make people uncomfortable. Their blue words choke on the air of their ignorance. If anything, these people embarrass themselves by being so negative and judgemental. Humbleness is a classic style that never gets old. The best books in life are crisp with uncomfortable content.

I dream of making a living off of sharing these ideas and helping people feel heard and safe. I will eventually make enough money to be independent and to help the community. I could live in a bigger city where I can go to more writers events, I could do more activism volunteering at more soup kitchens, with more people I can help and enjoy my time with. I dream of helping create a revolution. Every day; I wake up and I'm like ... huh; I hope so and so creates a revolution. I think to myself what can I do currently to help start a revolution. Which means no wage slavery, equal pay, equity, free healthcare. Ive volunteered in soup kitchens il'vegiven out free paintings and items to the homeless on the street. I've boycotted some stores. I've done phone banking in

Equality, Florida and for the democracy

organization of St. Lucie county. I am a

volunteer at Planned parenthood. I am

now a member of the African liberation

party, the uhuru movement.

It's ok if you have a different opinion on life.

This is for those who struggle to make a

community based on religious

intolerance to creative, intellectual

people, people who are neurodivergent,

people who are mentally ill, physically

disabled people who are queer or too

dark-skinned for people's liking or all of

the above. If trying to stay in a church or

christian family brings you distress, then

this is for you.

I noticed that when I was praying; I was just

answering to myself, and that I was

making an answer because I

desperately wanted to hear from god. In

some African spiritualities, Black people

practice atheism through viewing

themselves as their own deities. In

some ways, I believe I am a god as

much as everyone else is a god. We

create our own lives; we invent things,

and we come up with our own solutions.

This is like magic.

In Barbados, there is no such thing as a good morning. We greet by saying, "mourning". In the (mourning) morning. I mourn for my ancestors. I sing for my ancestors. I use positive chants and slave hymns. This makes me feel connected with my ancestors to feel whole and loved. It's up to each and everyone of us to decide what our own atheism looks like. I rely on community and my ability to feel close with people rather than talk to a wall and expect an answer from god, in fact the reason some Christians are happier is that they can fit in with the church and hang with the people there as a community not because of talking to himself and expecting an answer. But there are many people who

can't fit in with the church. Queer people

used to be deemed gods and goddesses

and emperors. They don't want us to know

our worth, they don't want us to know we

are gods, be it symbolic or not. We are

meant to feel big and powerful, not small

and insignificant.

Blind faith in religion has led to major

monstrosities across the world, including

queerphobia. Therefore I practice

atheism. I noticed in church they refused

to help queer people financially and to

let them contribute within the higher

positions of the church such as

preacher, bishop, deacon, and

sometimes the choir. And when they have a queer person in the church, that person must never talk about the issues that Queer people face, these people can't talk about queer acceptance. The churches I went to constantly put down queer people and did not want them to grow or have any type of popularity. Ive been to 10 churches in total and they have all been the same. People saying I shouldn't be born, shunning ostracizing me, telling me I shouldn't be gay, telling me I am the devil. People say that it's not all churches just because they feel like the church can't afford any criticism that if they defend the church, they will go to heaven. Why go to a place that does not welcome you? I took back my power and stop believing in Abrahamic religions. I don't have to worry about going to hell if I don't believe in hell. I can get out of the church and find a better hobby and career that is welcome to a wider audience.

Abrahamic religions are basically when the losers become at the top by manipulation, but this doesn't always work out. The losers of the world are the people who fail in evolution who are abusive, mean and intolerant of their environment and people around them.

In Christianity, it is deemed bad for people to rebel and retaliate against oppressors. It's insane the local pastor would usually tell us to love Hitler. The church seems to show more love for hitler than for Queer people, causing division between many black families and their Queer relatives. We are told it's wrong to feel the natural feeling of hate and rage. But when a person wants to oppress someone in the name of religion, such as Queerphobia, Misogyny, colonization and white supremacy, it is justified to show rage and hateful, sometimes violent, actions under the name of religion. When a slave attacks their master, he is punching up and should be supported at all costs. Mind you, that the prison industrial complex with the majority Black and BIPOC are kept as slaves to create most of our items and food out of free labour. Our taxes go to the police paycheck and we pay the police to murder and arrest us. We have to pay taxes for the military to kill darker-skinned people and palestinian people in Gaza and apartheids across the country. With all the major atrocities of the world, there is Christianity that tells us to shut up about it, to be docile and complicit.

18

Atheism is a belief that there is not a god, but other cultures are adapting by making values, connections, and hobbies as a higher power. For example, my higher power might be community or art. There is a new direction of atheism in the black community where people replace social science and political science with Christianity, saying, "if Jesus/god exists, then why didn't he help us when we were enslaved?" There is a type of theism movement going on and it's called the mental health atheist movement, where people are diagnosed with psychosis when they are going on religious rampages and delusions. People can now take medications instead of relying on an imaginary god to make themselves feel better.

I have a dream that there will be therapy and mutual aid where people put up tables and share printed papers of mental health topics on happiness and how to deal with stress, the skepticism of a god and what is psychosis. There will be buildings where people get mental health topics and basic biology topics and Ted talks instead of preaching the bible.

We need a new class of atheists and a new class of leftists. We need to talk in ways for the poor people to understand us. Atheists must abstain from being bourgeois and uppity. We must focus on giving free items, information and housing. We must focus on helping people stay happy and independent about how to share care and give to one another. Instead of making people feel dumb and insecure, we should meet people where they are at. We must remove racism and colorism from the scientist and atheist community. We need to talk about the BIPOC contributions toward inventions and science. We need to stop putting an emphasis on degrees because the United States hired random uneducated white people to do jobs in the white house and federal systems, white collar work and they learned the skills afterward. They restricted these jobs for white people only so that they could control the BIPOC. So we must use this way of recruitment and community building. We need unqualified and qualified black people together. We must hire first and worry about the job skills later!

mutual aid

• Safe space mutual aid is giving things like LGBTQ including ebook books, paintings, and accessories, in order to keep the spirit of pride even though pride is not on that day. This way, people can be themselves.

• erotica mutual aid, offering free nudes and erotic paintings, erotica books, free condoms, and pregnancy tests. Free.

• Black Pride Mutual Aid, sending newspapers, magazines, artwork with Black pride, inclusive black power, pan African messages. giving this free stuff to black people and other races who are receptive to this is powerful.

• erotica mutual aid is important for creating an environment of expression and Queer friendly spaces.

Democracy Mutual aid

Implementing and suggesting that people in a work environment, or peers, vote through raising of hands, vote through standing up. This is direct democracy, by mutual aid. It directly disrupts structures of work, school and group therapy/ support groups through giving access to voting. Democracy mutual aid is intimate direct democracy given in mutual aid without the influence of the state and federal systems.

We should have access to decisions on what we learn in school, what books we read, how the light bill is being billed, whether we should receive a light bill or charge for rent, we should decide what we eat during the day, we should decide what we want to talk about, and how we want to conduct ourselves

Asking the people to vote for what candy or snack you want to give them within the budget. This gives people control and

agency through democracy and the

pleasure of mutual aid. Giving options

for votes direct Democratic mutual aid is

to give the right social conditions for a

revolution.

Anarchical Decentralized Voting system

1. Make a vote on an issue and the person
   or people who lose in the vote has the
   say. If this demand can not work, they
   can be put in different groups with
   similar issues.

2. Finding the minority group example
   (Queer BIPOC) inclusion with any
   concern and having them come together

to bring up concerns. Once each individual comes up with an answer to how the problem will be addressed, then the minority group will vote amongst themselves, including. The boss must make sure the command is being fulfilled.

3. Voting for who represents the most oppressed groups and then letting them be the leader

Constant gift giving: in fort Mose there were frequent circulations of goods, services and customs, through different counties, they called it gift giving and even when there wasn't a trade to make they would

still give gifts for showing love.

How many commodities do we have? How

many commodities do we give? How

much do we buy? How many

commodities do we produce?

Sometimes we can clear out our closet

and give mutual aid to strangers.

Going into many black decentralized

groups, groups sometimes separate

from other races in which one mingles

and trades gifts and services peacefully,

is a form of black pride. Being able to

integrate with other races without

showing malice to the black community

is a form of black pride.

Class consciousness is difficult. People of

color of all races and ethnicities

separate into their own groups out of

necessity for emotional and physical

safety. Attempting to have a humanist

love for all that is alive to attempt to

sometimes mingle and to give gifts to

other races of people is a sign of

strength and power. True democracies

allow people to form their own groups,

without fees, fines, and dog whistles.

Indigenous tribe and Black slaves who

escaped formed intimate direct

democratic societies in fort Mose

cherokee tribes

The cherokee tribes,

Tried their best to deal with troublemakers,

they tried to give them a voice so those

who did not get along can advocate for

their needs to dissolve their trauma,

when things didn't work out with those

people the makers, went into different

local decentralized groups to find

community and to seek therapy and

wellness same could be done with

criminals. We can have criminals be

heard for what they need and if things don't work out, then they can be put into decentralized groups where they can find new community and therapy and love.

Small clusters of Queer communities are founded upon decentralization. It is the need to know that queer people need a place to live how they want to live, so should everyone else.

Me growing up as a queer person needs a safe place to be as queer as I want to be and if I don't have that space I am more overt than the time of place because I am used to not finding anywhere else I can be myself. When I eventually found my group, I slowly became more adjusted to knowing a time and place and being flaming in the groups that called for it.

I noticed that places that were carefree were more queer friendly. People that minded their own business on what was appropriate or not. What they felt was weird or not, usually were more accepting of queer people. I noticed that spaces that talked about positive experiences being Queer had more positive reactions far more than topics that discussed the struggles in the queer community. Spaces that

encouraged for Queer people to live authentic

lives and to be happy thrived. Topics on the

need for Mental/physical health care plus

anatomy and how it contributes to success in

family and careers. People who had positive

out looks on queer people had openly queer

family members and wanted their family

members to be happy.

Groups are competitive toward one another

from groups that are distributed into pies.

Anything that disrupts the status quo creates

competition and chaos. Not doing anything to

disrupt the status quo of capitalism can cause malus. Everyone needs to learn how to coexist with one another in their lives.

Culture can change with time. It is a type of violence to disrupt smaller groups from forming and new identities to persist. This violence stops the natural progression of human life. In a democracy, we need decentralized groups.

I learned that if I wanted to implement democracy into my space; I needed to give people the right to ruin their lives and make the wrong decisions. Some people innately want to feel sad, some people want to get into trouble and do hard drugs. Telling people to stop will change nothing. If we lived a life where we controlled everyone's choice, then that would lead to a hostile environment. People going to prison over trivial issues is what we need to end.

Democracy Mutual aid is for people to experience the right social conditions for a revolution.

PIE DISSECTION

Decentralized democracy pie dissection calls for people to split off into groups on political issues and experiences by a survey while mingling with common ground. For example, in LGBTQIA organizations split in groups on 1 to 3 issues, for example, who prioritizes intersectionality of people of color, who prioritizes disability visibility, who prioritize prison industrial complex Abolition, who prioritizes each of them by order and see who is a match. Then split off into abilities such as drawing, painting, digital art, photography, Quotes, poetry, card making. The goal is for the person in this pie dissected group to help teach these other people new skills, and use it to create art that can be given to strangers as mutual aid.

This disrupts the status quo because privileged people dislike unity. They do not want people with common issues to come together and get things done. Drama filled people thrive on chaos and isolation. Have you ever been in a group of people and felt alone? We need people to come together that are not out of identity politics alone because all it will do is cause trauma bonding and emptiness. We need LGBT LGBTs to come together by important values such as equal housing, free health care, PIC abolition, and taxing the rich.

When tensions of structural racism are left unhealed and are not addressed,then there are eruptions of anger to appear. Or black people and BIPOC may just walk out and not show up

to LGBTQ events. This happens way too often.

We need class consciousness and solidarity.

Not learning healthy ways to point out

differences leads to racism.

In pie dissection people become territorial and

want to dissect the pie into smaller groups

debating which belief is supreme of them all in

the given space. I call this the evolution

process when groups pile up new ideas and

adapt to shape another idea.

Boundaries need not be Barriers: Leading

Collaboration among Groups in Decentralized

Organizations.

Page 1 - 4

SLUSH PIE

In this territorial process the can be a phenomenon when groups transform their actions and identities to form new connections with groups that once broke off, perhaps the peers have walked off with a new skill. When ideology is suppressed and actions are made the value of its core principles new peers are accepted in the in group more than previous attempts. When the outsider is reflected back by similar role models shown to groups and when the outsider is pushed to a leadership position the evolution process begins in my argument contrary to the concern of groups becoming too cliquey and territorial.

It is the broader shared interests and the groups ability for the goal to be achieved, that brings people closer together to broader

shared beliefs like free health care. Food and

housing.

When there is praise of the skill of collaboration

the groups become less hostile. Skills of

everyone in the group must be recognized. The

groups work with ease when it is focused on

working with ease instead of advocating for

improvement.

When the group is decided right for you it is

important to focus on positive affirmations and

collaborative efforts

Boundaries need not be Barriers: Leading

Collaboration among Groups in Decentralized

Organizations.

Page 5- 14

I don't believe in segregation. I believe in Autonomy for Black people to do as they please and to go in and out of spaces they are not welcome. I don't want to be around white people who see me as less than and call me a monkey because I know I am none of those things. It shouldn't make people mad that I want to be in a place where I am loved and appreciated or to be with people who look like me, especially when I sometimes go to other races of people. Black people are the only group of people that get mad that they want to choose if they want to be close to their own race and people get mad when they want to know their ancestry. This happens to no other race and african americans are the only racial group whose roots in ancestry have been erased. What's with the contradiction? Do these people not want black people to be happy? I don't know about you but I love my family and my ancestors. They gave me life and I am happy to be alive. If this offends a non black person then maybe they are an enemy who doesn't want my well being. If you are non black and you feel happy for us black people then great you are welcome. This book is for all people including white people and thank you to the black hispanic,south asian, east asian, and white people who helped me in my life.

We deserve the rights of the City. Why does a funky Orange corporate clown in a blue suit get to tell us what to do? Why is it we can't decide whether we get a light bill? Why can't we own the water and food that every other species in the animal kingdom has for free? Why can't Native Americans and the blacks own the water of America? I deserve to decide whether I'm either getting or building a free house that is made for me to live in. If people are going through abuse with their family, they should be able to simply build their own house to live in. We deserve to be relieved of these stupid rules and taxes so we can rent a home. Most of us can't even dream of getting a mortgage.

Why don't we control what type of business is in our city? What type of bookstores, cafes and bars do we have? We want mental hospitals and programs that talk about generational,

racial trauma and harmful habits. We want

programs to teach children, teens, and adults

how to plant and use a farm that includes all

races of people. We want to learn ways to stay

safe from one another.

WE DESERVE THE RIGHTS TO OUR BODIES AND THE RIGHTS TO THE CITY

When I was in school, us kids wanted sex ed,

and we were grown enough to consume

grown-up content from the age of 12 to 13. We

wanted to learn how to be independent adults

not kept in a cocoon. We want the right to our

bodies and the rights to the city. We want to

control how the country or county reacts to our

body. We want parts of land that are split by the natural progression of culture, not by stagnation.

We deserve to have an Autonomy of our bodies. Women deserve to have a say on whether they have an abortion and should have one if they choose.

Us queer people deserve to have children and to adopt.

THE LUMPENPROLETARIAT

The lumpenproletariat is often criticized in a

negative light by Karl Marx but Marx was like

many writers a product of their time, we can

see the through the complexities of data within

history stone wall and the civil rights

revolutions that disabled, rugged street

dwellers were the core of the movements.

They are the working class but do not work the

same way as what is conventional or the norm.

Casual laborers, the peasants, the undeserving

poor, the marginalized, and they are liberated

for their non-conformity; these are gay and

transgender people and immigrants.

Marx says ignorance influence

lumpenproletariat to recruit as soldiers against

the proletariat

I argue that not all of them have chosen that

route. Many of these bottom dwellers are more

quick to militarize against police and state

powers. It is their feeble aggression and rage

that fuels these movements. Lumpenproletariat

doesn't have much to lose that are in constant

attacks from police force and state violence.

The lumpenproletariat is a dangerous class at

best.

ANALYSIS OF STONE WALL

In stonewall Marsha P Johnson is shown to

take the clothes right off her back when a

stranger on the street said they liked the way

she looked.

As a Marxist analysis, the lumpen proletariat

must give out the little belongings they have

as a constant mutual aid to dismantle the bitter

politics of bourgeois therapist's advice. That

says, take care of yourself before taking care

of someone else. I argue staying bitter alone

and hoarding the smallest items you have left

will not save you. It is the evolution of the

animal kingdom and the human species where

fewer animals give mutual aid that learns to

thrive more than the animals on top of the food chain.

Using the master's tools of selfishness and profit doesn't help anyone. Anyone, despite mental health struggles, physical impairment deserves to feel the love and warmth to give and to receive back. I noticed my low self esteem made me not see when people were giving back to me when I was giving mutual aid by accident. I was in one of the most chaotic churches of plant a seed ministry. In this ministry, on probation, I gave out tons of items I had and because of this, people from other homes defended me when the church bullied me, when people tried to physically harm me out of the blue. I noticed how I changed the

moral code of the white majority church, that

church was not supposed to miss a Black

transgender identified person by unwritten

rules of capitalist structures. People walked up

to me to say, wow we missed you. I'm sure

people often thought, "Why is this black queer

person with little money giving out more things

than this church?" Why is it that this pastor has

manicures and the houses we live in have

holes and bed bugs?

HOW TO BEAT THE MASTER'S TOOLS OF CHARITY

There have been many times where churches denied me mutual aid because I wanted what they gave out. Not only that, I felt I had to be self conscious and in fear so I kept my sexuality under wraps because I was afraid of churches neglecting me as they often did to me. I now understand that the church gives constant charity and free supplies in order to have the power to restrict those commodities and services to LGBTQ people and BIPOC of different classes and identities from the norm.

In order to beat this is to be selfless. It is to give and serve others. I Preserve my energy when needed too but I keep giving after I recharge. I noticed to never complain about giving people things and never be an Indian giver. When you kill people with kindness, you ignore and disengage from their ignorance. They will absolutely love you and you will disrupt the system.

The oppressors want us to become an empty shell of ourselves; the structures want us to close off in shame. Keep loving people. The more you give to people, the more you make an environment easier to decentralize your social life without so many bullies.

When the time comes for it brings up the contradictions of the church's behavior because most churches will only give out loaves of bread, if not dust, while living in Teslas and sports cars.

I am a member of the Uhuru movement because I believe in black pride. I like a combination of centralist and decentralist ideas. I like both ideas and that there is not just one way of doing things. However, when black movements are under intense FBI attack at some point, one of their decisions might be to decentralize their groups. I believe that decentralized black pride/ decentralized black power groups are very empowering. When there are basic rules illegal to not be proletariat, and making colonialism and imperialism illegal.

UHURU MOVEMENT

The uhuru movement taught me we should

search and demand an end to colonialism

instead of racism because white people

understand that colonialism harms themselves.

White people don't understand racism. We can

all agree that white people should stop

interfering with other foreign countries,

bombing, raping, creating genocide of people

of color.

Why is punching up limitations on freedom, ok?

Freedom is an illusion. In America, we often

punch down. The U.S. punches down through

laws like taxing barter systems criminalizing

socialism and boycotts criminalizing free

healthcare. Freedom is a constant illusion. It is

whether we decide to punch up or punch down

for restrictions. I believe in decentralized

Democracies with African centrist

values/principles. Don't get me wrong? I love

African democratic centralism. What I'm saying

is that once African centralism is successful in

it enlargement people naturally call for

decentralized group breaking up into

increments, queer black areas of the city,

womanist areas of the city, nudist areas of the

city, economic issues can split off such as

whether a person can decide to make their

own home for free without taxes,

criminalization and private property ownership

as one can in many African countries.

True democracy is letting others be who they truly want to be.

Why don't we have civilizations like this today?

Colonization wiped out most civilizations because of their superior military force. There were more violent and male dominated, such as the Mayans that were destroyed from imperialism as well,

MY DREAM

My dream is that there will be a smaller voting group of minorities to decide for America. I dream that within the jobs we have, we can make votes among our employees on what the job can take part in and for employees to vote

on what manager and CEO should be hired
and fired.

When I was in Publix working as a bagger,
stocker and janitorial worker. We went into a
meeting, and we talked about buying stocks
and our wealth increasing. I then started
wondering what if we voted for our own CEOs
and managers in the meetings. What if we
decided about the items and food we helped
sell in the stores? What if we owned segments
of the store and land?

African countries such as southern Sudan and
Uganda have tribes in which people make their

own houses out of clay without any taxes and rent. In America we have more education on how to design and make a home. We could have volunteers and friends who can help us make a house. I dream that one day we won't have any laws, taxes, loans, mortgages and payments for making a house. Imagine getting kicked out of a home for being Queer, or living in a place you are being abused dont want to be then being able to make your own home so you don't have to be homeless

I remember days me and my sister would fight as children and my parents pretended they were the judge as we roleplay and to figure things out instead of actually calling for legal help we became each others help and this is something ide like to see more of.

Feminist Syndicalism

I dream that there would be matriarch syndicalism, where blue collar jobs and various other professions will be purposely passed down to women and their children. Special raises and offers would be given to daughters so that women can have more autonomy. I realized that if my mom didn't have autonomy I would not have been born from a lesbian mom. many world issues and crimes against humanity are caused because women lack autonomy.

Matriarch Syndicalism is were wealth and labor is passed down through cis het women and queer women. It is policies and benefits from trade jobs that give free employment and education to women and trade jobs that pass down from the mother as options.

This makes it easier for women to find independence and flourish away from domestic abuse.

Third Space Safespace

I would write what was said by the survey and why I chose to make that rule in the school, in the job and in the club/ group. I have dreams of playing a game where. I would converse with people about positive laws we would want for everyone and then we could write it down and take a picture of it with the address of where we could make an invisible landmark. In theatre class of high school and ROTC class I learned how role playing can manipulate the current situation which then can lead to a

future outcome. We could write on paper what
we want the environment/safe S to be

I dream that we would draw a line in chalk of a

small area and then write down positive laws

that we want to go by and make a place where

we do not have wage slavery using barter

systems between parties. Spaces that are very

queer friendly where we can dress where we

want, talk like how we want.

Third space safe space is made out of defiance
of harsh conditions and the need to escape
into a world of utopia. This leftist third space is
usually made by vigilantes and street dwellers.
People who are going through tough lives and
situations, kicked out of homes for being
Queer.

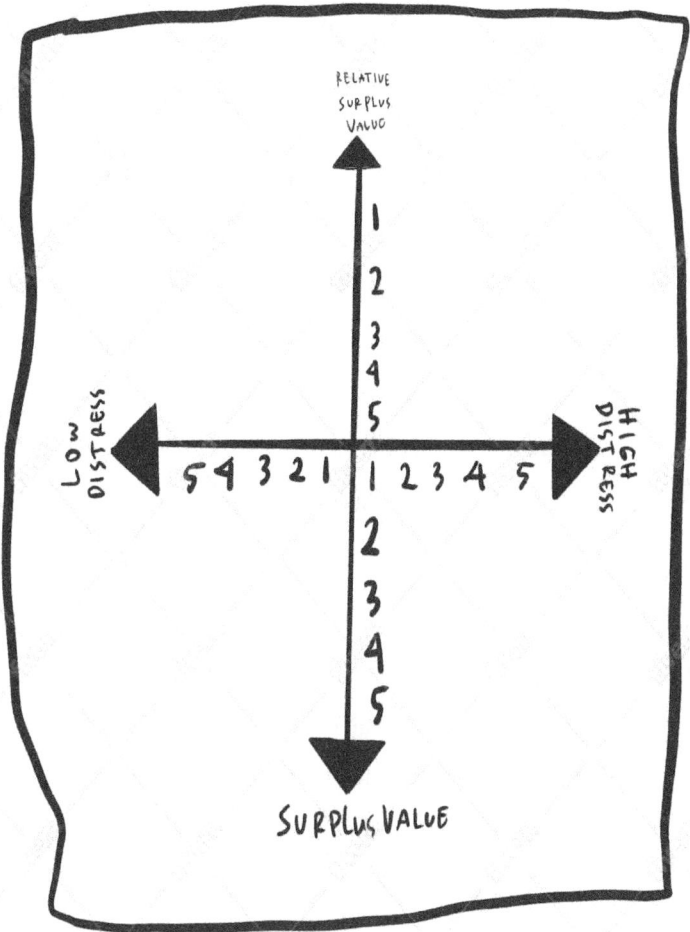

- (green) Today
- (red) sometimes

- (brown) most times
- (Blue) all the time

"In Marxist economics, relative surplus value refers to the surplus labor extracted by capitalists from workers through increased productivity and the resulting reduction in the value of labor-power (wages). Unlike absolute surplus value, which is extracted by simply lengthening the working day, relative surplus value is derived from shortening the necessary labor time needed to reproduce the worker's labor-power. This is achieved by increasing the productivity of labor through technological advancements and other methods that reduce the amount of time needed to produce the means of subsistence."

Absolute surplus value is produced when a worker is forced to work for longer hours than necessary to reproduce their own labor power, and the capitalist appropriates the surplus labor time. This is achieved by simply prolonging the working day, potentially at the cost of worker well-being.

Relative surplus value, on the other hand, is created through advancements in technology and the organization of labor, leading to higher productivity and a greater output of commodities in the same amount of time. This allows the capitalist to extract more surplus labor without necessarily extending the working day. For example, if a machine-driven factory can produce the same output in half the time, the capitalist can increase the surplus value without extending the working day, notes the Marxists Internet Archive.

How it works. Apply two dots of any color toward

the number of what applies to you. For example, on

the bottom is absolute surplus value on the top

relative surplus value. Green represents today, so if i

asked you how high is the absolute surplus value, i

will put the green dot on the highest number to the

bottom of the page if this is causing me medium

amount of distress i would put the green dot farther

to the right under the number three. If i was asked

about relative surplus value my dot would be higher

above and the color would differe depending on the

days

In capitalist countries food is not spoiled but is to be

destroyed over greed. Employees are paid to work

overtime to produce these items, and then they're also underpaid. With more labor time, if pants cost 45 dollars a part time, the employee should be paid $45.00 per pants. If the employee makes 4 pants that day for 3 hours a day for 3 days a week for 4 weeks in 1 month, that would equal 6,480 a month.

3 hours (3h), 3 days (3d), 4 weeks in a month (4W).

$45.00 × 4 × 3h × 3d ×4w = 6,480 a month.

In capitalism, we are paid hourly $15.00 × 5h × 4d × 4w= $1,200 15 an hour times 5 hours times 4 days a week, 4 weeks a month, which is 1,200 a month. That is less than half of the money for working part time. In full time$15.00× 9h × 7d × 4w =$3,780 4w $15.00 an hour times 9 hours times 7 days times 4 weeks a month that would be $3,780 that is half the amount of money paid if labor was valued, with a substantial increase of unnecessary hours.

Overall, in a better economy where people are paid what they are worth, they would have a substantially higher earning wage and more leisure time. Here we can see that schizophrenic people and autistic people are not lazy; they just have a hard time competing with the high labor value and wage exploitation. In many circumstances, it is the societal influences that give a schizophrenic and autistic person stress, society needs to change. It is this structure of society that lowers the quality of life of the schizophrenic patient. If people with severe mental illness were paid what they deserve through a barter system, ultimately there would be less stress in their lives and they would have equal access to freedom and upward mobility. Disabled

people deserve to be paid more than those who are

not, because their anguish and extra hard work to do

the same tasks that a neurotypical person does,

definitely this would benefit the life of the

disadvantaged, disabled people achieve above and

beyond what is required when there is an

opportunity for them to work at their own paise.

The economic exploitation of neurodivergent

people dismantles relationships with neurotypicals

and their own neurodivergent peers. The economic

oppression and high surplus value makes the quality

of life by neurodivergence different from the

neurotypical. The development and progression of

life by disabled people is thus regressed to difficulty

in their mobilizing of the world. This further

alienates non-disabled people from different abled bodies and neurotypical individuals. The perceived lack of social and emotional benefits of being in the presence of a neurodivergent person invokes the severely mentally ill individual to be subject to objectification, followed by pity and repulsion when the disabled person does not meet up the expectations of perfection. Since structural influences skewer the relationship such as low economic competition, the neurotypical person may look to shallow descriptions of what makes them value that disabled person, such as body type, or popularity to make up for the disabled person's shortcomings. The neurotypical expects the neurodivergent to accept the depiction of working twice as hard to shed away stigma. The neurodivergent is expected to break a sweat to keep

up with the wandering eyes that land upon their

stigma to cover up with academic and goal

achievement leading to depletion of mental health

One might then cater to the gaze from the

perpetually privileged criticizer the person desires

to please, or the neurodivergent individual may

choose to abstain from all objectification and

display disdain for anyone who crosses the

boundary. Some people may objectify themselves to

escape from not entirely meeting up to society's

norms. Can cause society's achievement or class

clown behavior. Or we can live in a life where we

work for the benefit of the community without

money or a currency. Trading goods between parties

with Barter systems.

There is an error in perception to revert to

infantilization of neurodivergent people in order to

escape pity and objectification. Surely Autistic and

schizophrenic people are worthy of being put on a

pedestal. However, domestic courtship, and raising

children costs money and the hardships that the

neurodivergent person faces increases stigma. With

the progression of society and the benefits it gives

to disabled people, marriage and family raising

becomes more accessible and valuable to the

neuro-divergent person and those who admire them.

SSI can be inherited through married partners and

their children through what is called survivors'

benefits. Being on SSI

A counselor of mine for disabled people had an autistic child. The kids did not want to play with him; she said she hoped for him to one day go to college. She had big dreams for him and that she just needed to accept the fact that he might never meet the requirements; she went on and said I just need to keep helping my son. Either he does or not; she persists to say; I don't like it when people use the word high functioning and low functioning because saying those phrases sound like it is perpetuating a hierarchy. It makes me feel like they are saying to me and my son is garbage! Lesser than!. I said, yeah once you think about that, I would like to be put in the category of high functioning and lower functioning. It sounds objectifying as well as scientific and unfairly analytical of hierarchical differences. She further sobbed as she saw him want to play with the kids. So I went and played with him. I had a close.

A friend sees no more who crashes into my apartment now and then. He was Schizoaffective, like me, yet he was autistic. I later found out he was homeless and addicted to drugs. One night he went to my house in the winter with baggy clothes filled with bruises and I thought I must invent something to help somebody.

It is the constant pressure for climbing a ladder, competing, materialism and social Darwinism that fosters an environment for hatred. Encouraged by my parents growing up, I gave the homeless people money, food and even volunteered for the community. I later volunteered in soup kitchens, where I stocked the food and packaged the hot supper after coming home from work. It is these experiences that influence those to be less ableist and to not internalize ableism.

The plan is to work in steps to achieve an anarchist world. If everything was given freely and traded through a barter system then there wouldn't be as many hierarchies. Imagine how much value

someone is seen for having a nice house or being

able to afford to pay for a gift to give someone.

When commodities are free and through traid of

another commodity neither parties are losing in the

exchange. Gratitude is then expanded to a great

magnitude of expression by one another.

Chapter 3 how I became confident

Opulence, neurotypical opulence, and

neurodivergent opulence.

Opulence is defined as wealth, affluence, and

abundance.

The reaction to fetishism of neurodivergence can be

harmful. This creates, sense of neurotypical

opulence which takes play in the course of our lives.

It is the process of me splitting my sense of self into

many pieces to be easily digestible to the

neurotypical world. One might do so while

masking, it is the act of attempting an exaggerated

mirroring and strategizing to fit into the norm of the

gender norm, racial and or class norms. It is the

extreme shame and guilt of one's true identity of

natural, genuine, and authentic true self. Splitting

myself in the overreliance of persona and demeanor,

rather than likes and dislikes, personal experiences,

achievements, values, and an authentic community.

This sense of intense mirroring without the ability for one's true self to bring to the surface that can lead to confusion of life, and inner dread. In my intense mirroring on the mask I might have brief periods of silence giving the signal of body language, "im stiff, imperfect, I'm not moving see if I freeze there can't be problems." Conformity to neurotypical opulence can lead to shutting down and the replaying of negative circumstances and the dissociation from what the person truly wants in life. One might even lose more of the ability of whom to see as a threat in their lives and who to avoid, and who to associate with. Neurotypical opulence can make the neurodivergent person feel every negative encounter is their fault and can be avoided if they try harder. They may even try to up

their status among their group of negatively
influential peers by being a bully, getting in trouble
and/ or being a class clown.

Neurodivergent opulence is about saying I am
neurodivergent ... but I am...? I'm
neurodivergent... So?... it is an act of thriving and
resilience. Yes, it's important that I am
Neurodivergent, but I am also an athlete and or
artist, for example. Not putting so much emphasis
on gender norms and labels, some might do so and
still claim their assigned gender identity that was
given to them at birth. One might indulge in
neurodivergent opulence by letting achievements be
known, showing off muscle growth when there is
the right time and place, showing people how many

pushups you can do, showing off discipline skills

such as punctuality, tucking in the bed during the

morning. Showing parts of ourselves that are

positive to others reflects a positive self image that

strengthens. This certainly has worked for me.

HOW I MADE A QUEER VIGILANTE

• Vigilantism is the act of preventing,

investigating, and punishing perceived offenses

and crimes without legal authority. When I first

went to the church, I thought of jail and how to

survive. I thought of how to find someone who can protect me by creating queer vigilantes and peaceful vigilantes.

• when in a hostile environment, the visibly queer person will either meet four types of protectors. The solidarity protector, the king protector, the sugar daddy protector, the mother protector. People who protect queer people the most are past incarcerated people and non biased mental health professionals. People in jail who end up liking Trans women protect them at all costs. It is the comradery of prison culture, class struggle, and fetish that feeds the queer vigilantes needed to protect queer people. vigilantes don't need a label or even a uniform. Vigilantes are a way of behavior comradery. Criminals or past criminals who are lumpenproletariat are not afraid of doing crimes, been in and out of jail are those who become vigilantes.

• The solidarity protector usually unified with me under the sentiment that the 1% ruling class wants us to fight among each other to distract from exploitation so that we don't eat. Among black people there is a collective understanding that race comes before all and so I say white want us black people to fight among each other, the rich want to keep racism alive so we don't point to the rich so the ruling class can keep the money and stop us from eating. When there are people of Un intellectual groups, I keep it short to say white supremacy wants us black people to attack

each other. As I started getting butch... girl, I

don't know why maybe my hormones changed

as I got in my 20s.

• for people to protect me. I become selfless

and give constantly. I disengage with

arguments. I preach love and peace when the

time and place call for it. I stop gossiping. I

state I don't gossip; I promote peace and love. I

tell people I can't fight the world and that I want

to stay safe, but I can't do it alone. Like Marsha

p Johnson, I give things in a constant way. I

also work out among men and I ask them for

self defense tips. I make sure that I never

question the man's sensuality or

heterosexuality at all. To keep mutual respect. I

may even feed into that idea if that's what he identifies as so that he can respect my identity and protect me.

• the king protector is the man who wants servitude in order to boost his ego needs, and social status as he protects you. He is supposed to be considered the strong, secure man with conceitedness. He wants you to give him massages, lend him things and share food. Praise him as a king. This person can sometimes ask for sexual favors, but keep in mind that sexual favors can make the relationship more complicated and lead to an end of support. Some king protectors also might be ok when you turn them down.

• The sugar daddy is like the king, but this person is more possessive and usually their boundaries change from rigid to no boundaries at all. These people can be dangerous because they give these things to possess me or to control me.

• The mother protector is a cisgender woman or another Trans woman who puts you under her wing and she introduces you to womanhood or what she learned from her gay uncles. She usually protects Trans women who look manly or show attractive boyish traits. This is because most cisgender women, even as allies, still view Trans women's secrets from men and that her mother's instincts come out when she sees a little boy that needs to be

protected.

• Peaceful vigilantes are people who use acts

of intimidation, body size, commanding voices

and sometimes verbal threats when needed to

protect the queer people in the community.

Peaceful vigilantes serve as guards.

•. When I was in church, I asked some people

to protect me. I told them the truth about how

the police took advantage of me when I called

for their help when I needed someone and that

I felt alone and in fear. I told the surrounding

people I loved them and that I needed them. I

often said thank you and you're welcome. I

also cleaned and did my chores too. I even

gave gifts and bought friends my age and older

than me candy and a drink. We looked after

each other as a community. I reminisced about

comradery through prison by making jokes

about being jailbait. I gave an even amount of

sense of protection because I was a big guy, so

I served as a natural guard often because I

was naturally protective of LGBTQ and people

of color because I don't want people to hurt like

I did. I often told them how the police took

advantage of me for being queer and disabled,

we can't trust the police and all we have is us

queer people the shamed and the damned.. I

don't like for people to feel alone. I preached

the need to help the underdog. I said, if I were

in a house going on fire, would you try to save

you? Chad says," I don't know. I protested with

a laugh." I'd save you? Are you gonna just leave me? "Chad said in a calm voice. I gotta make sure I'm safe. I say true... true ... I know you care about me. I'm sure if it actually happened you might try to help me in real life and especially if the house isn't too burnt down. Chad says, yeah true I care about you.

• I needed to have trust in love and belonging to keep this going. I needed to rid myself of my fears and insecurities. During the time I struggled with getting the right medication, I was scared and isolated in a group home halfway house.

• What I dreamed of more than anything was to be surrounded by a new structure of government. Such as one that is run by mental health professionals and vigilantes. There is a constant interruption of mental health teams taking care of people by corporations being funded by right-wing groups. Mental health programs can't help everyone 24/7 LGBT people of color often exhaust these programs because they are under constant bullying and harassment. That's where vigilantes come in. These programs often come and go. Often ignorant politicians don't allow most of these programs to take place because they are OK with violence and suffering of the poor. Vigilantes support sentiments like to keep your hands to yourself, keep from danger and violence.

Mobile Crisis Teams (MCTs):

These teams, composed of mental health clinicians, behavioral health technicians, or peers, respond to mental health crises in the community, providing immediate stabilization and referrals to services.

Co-Responder Teams (CRTs):

These teams comprise mental health clinicians embedded within police agencies, who respond alongside law enforcement officers to calls involving people experiencing mental health crises.

Alternative Responder Programs:

These programs send social workers or

behavioral health specialists to call instead of

police officers

Crisis Intervention Teams (CITs):

While CITs are often police-based, they are

trained to de-escalate and divert individuals in

crisis to behavioral health services.

CAHOOTS (Crisis Assistance Helping Out On

The Streets):

This program, operating in Eugene, Oregon,

sends teams of a clinician and a medic to

respond to 911 calls police elsewhere deal with.

STAR (Support Team Assisted Response):

A similar program to CAHOOTS, also sends a medic and a crisis worker to respond to calls involving mental health, homelessness, and substance use.

What Happens When We Send Mental Health Providers Instead of Police - Vera Institute

May 27, 2021 — The Crisis Assistance Helping Out on the Streets (CAHOOTS) program pairs a medic with a crisis worker to respond to 911 and non-emergency calls ...

Vera Institute google AI

- I was minding my own business on the bus next to chad. crazy stranger says, I'm going to beat up this fag so bad!, the stranger said im going to deck him! Chad says, no the fuck you are not! I'll beat you up! I said how did you hear the conversation I said about my last partner. I was talking to a close friend, not you, quietly, too. Please mind your own business.? I was too scared to call the police. The members of the community removed him from the bus and out of the program. We were a group of people branded as criminals. We knew what it was like to feel alone, and there was no one outside to help us.

• In Florida, Section 741.30 of the Florida Statutes allows for a court to issue a protective injunction (often called a restraining order) in cases of domestic violence, which can include ordering the abuser to be excluded from the shared residence.

• My mom's partner has been emotionally and psychologically abusing me for years. My mom has joined the insults. My mom's partner told me I was a loser often. My biological mom said she wished she had aborted me on my birthdays. My moms wife would often beat my cousin in law for 15 minutes with fists and a belt, as they rolled on the floor screaming, my

moms wife often did this as a demonstration of

what she wanted to do to me, she often said

she wanted to spank me like she did them,

since I was 13 to 18 years old. My mom's wife

often blamed me for everything that went

wrong, she blamed my mom's aging, and her

arthritis, my moms partner often kept me in

fear, guilt, and shame. My mom's girlfriend

often said how I should suffer

Like her and that I should be homeless. I have

learning disorders, though I'm above average

in other areas. I have schizoaffective bipolar,

depressive type. I was poor, somewhat

affluent, and born into an ignorant family. I did

not know of the resources and the online

reports I could have used. With the help of therapists and social workers, I learned how to articulate myself and how to seek help. I was born into a small-minded family and so I thought small I didn't think there were resources to look up online. I didn't know where to begin. I often told my teachers that I think I have a mental illness and that my family is abusing me. The teachers told me I was big and black and that I shouldn't be scared and that I don't need help. I felt that smaller white people could kill me together or atleast one and that the police will say that I was big and black so I must have done something wrong. Many people would take the side of the smaller white person. I can't hit back because people will call the police and arrest me. I can't leave a

mark because people will say I'm the

aggressor. I felt like an isolated big black

monster on a hill the city comes to to put me in

a cage and poke me with their sticks. My

mom's partner one time pinned me to the

ground, and my head hit the floor as I saw

stars. My mom's partner put little effort as she

was way stronger than me. She was huge and

butch. When I was 18, she chased me around

the house saying she would kill me and I

picked up a knife and called the police. The

police said a bunch of racist jokes saying I

didn't do nuffin. They said I was big and black

and that I didn't need protection. They told me

and my mom they were taking me to a mental

hospital, New Horizons Midway, and they sent me to jail instead. They did not make it so that disabled people and other minorities who have conflict with family have to be removed from the home. The way they remove people from the home is by taking them to jail/prison. I've met women and men affected by this law and many black people walk away with a false criminal record coming back to their abusers unable to be independent from those toxic family members because they have felonies which restrict employment and higher wage opportunities. housing discriminated against those with felonies. I know black women who were domestically abused, but since the men were the one with a scratch, they have been arrested. I know men who were big and black, so the police believed the women when they said they were being abused by them. this bill helps no one. it is contradictory. the police department of Florida does nothing but keep black people in the cycle of abuse and isolation. It's been 10 years and I've dealt with micro aggressions and profiling in job interviews. I've done remote jobs because I don't want to be treated less than. I don't need these people to lower my self esteem. My bio mom was often nurturing and sweet. She helped and gave to everyone. My mom often tried to coddle me so badly it looked like abuse. she often sank into mood swings and depression and she threw glass bottles at our heads as we ducked.

•

I say this to my friends: I can choose to be bitter, I can wish everyone I come across to be incarcerated or I can be a better person and wish people well. The same things I can get someone arrested for are the crimes I could get arrested over profiling for something I didn't do. The prison industrial complex is a business that runs on our fear, resentment, and grief. It's up to me if I want to heal and engage with the community in a meaningful way.

.

www.ingramcontent.com/pod-product-compliance
Lightning Source LLC
Chambersburg PA
CBHW020709270326